THE UNMAKING

Tim O'Leary grew up in Witshire and lives in London. He began his career as an archaeologist in England, Wales and Tunisia before becoming a photographer. His poems have been shortlisted in competitions including Live Canon, Munster Lit Fest, Poetry on the Lake and Strokestown International. He won Cork's Hungry Hill Wild Atlantic Words in 2015. His work has appeared in *Allegro, And Other Poems, Ink Sweat and Tears, Poetry Salzburg Review* and *The High Window*, as well as several anthologies. The sequence *Manganese Tears* was published in the Poetry Salzburg Pamphlet series in late 2018.

THE UNMAKING

Tim O'Leary

The High Window

First published in the UK in 2019 by The High Window Press
3 Grovely Close
Peatmoor
Swindon
SN5 5SN
Email: abbeygatebooks@yahoo.co.uk

The right of Tim O'Leary to be identified as the author of this work has been asserted by him in accordance with Copyright, Designs and Patent Act, 1988.
© Tim O'Leary 2019
ISBN: 978-1-913201-07-4

All rights reserved. No part of this book may be reproduced or transmitted in any form or by any means, electronic or mechanical, including photocopying, recording, or by any information storage and retrieval system, without permission in writing from the copyright owner. This book may not be lent, hired out, resold or otherwise disposed of by way of trade in any form of binding or cover other than that in which it is published, without prior consent of the publishers.

Designed and typeset in Palatino Linotype
by The High Window Press.
Cover art: *Cells are Dividing* by Melanie O'Leary © 2019
Back cover photograph of Tim O'Leary by Jorge Arango Kure © 2019
Printed and bound by Lulu.com.

CONTENTS

All our gems have been worn before

North Meadow   11
Lent   12
An Elm at Halloween   13
Film on the Skyline   14
Echo Location   15
Ancestry   17
The Petals in the Snow   19
After the Wake   20
Paradigm Shift   21
Capo Palinuro   22
The Disposition of the Sun   24
Live Streaming   25
Straits of Messina   26
The Cortex Coast   27
The Medlar   28

The violet was flawed on the lawn

Still Frame   31
Clytie   32
Writing Down Passwords   33
In Exile   35
Above the Bay   36
False Dawn   37
Rail   38
Crux   39
Divine Works   40
Dawn in Accettura   41
Here Was Castro   42
Open Season, Valdichiana   43
The Moss House   45

Sunday in the Bleached Piazza 47
The Migrant 48

For all things change, making way for each other

Acts of Love 51
Clouds at Snape 52
At the Eye Hospital 53
The Workers 54
The Secret of Evensong 55
Green Belt 56
Writers in Marina Baixa 57
Nura 58
Heap Theory 59
Chess Garden 61
Tea in Maine 63
To the Land of Punt 65
Conquest 66

A Spell For Green Corn

Verse for the Marshes 69
Sea of Jazz 71
The Place of Stones 72
Yawarra 73
Butchery Lesson Before Easter 75
Behind a City Church 76
Son Running 77
Puck Fair 1959 78
Lament from Euganean Hills 79
The Photos at Avebury 81
Bats in Lucania 82
In The Morning… 83
Juniper Dune 84
Eve of Epiphany 85

Koyaanisqatsi — 'life of moral corruption or turmoil, life out of balance' *Hopi Dictionary: Hopiikwa Lavaytutuveni*. A state of life that calls for another way of living. As in the 1982 Godfrey Reggio film of the same name with music by Philip Glass.

'Well heaven forgive him! and forgive us all !
some rise by sin, and some by virtue fall ...'

Escalus in *Measure For Measure*, Act 2, Scene1

All our gems have been worn before

Louis MacNeice: 'Idle Talk' from *Solstices*

North Meadow

I need the alms of laughter
but go unheeded
in the dead unbeasted calm.

The inundation murmurs
as if I know no place.
Neither lord nor vassal,

you don't hold land from me,
I do not from you —
we have no polity.

The three-field system's gone,
earth of every furlong
drowning with the cow's lick.

Sky reflects flood reflects sky.
Politics of a feud finding
fealty, merely with time.

Lent

As days lengthen
bone bare branches
sap all strength.

Unsure penitents
in a guilty wilderness
that growth has left

but not abandoned
to the cursed virtue
of a fast enforced.

Two lovers flit through
early cherries, unflinching
in their itch for life:

are they future or past,
someone else or us?
Esoteric souls

too soon veiled by
a snow of blossom
beyond the dank verandah.

An Elm at Halloween

Dangling airless, the yellow balloon's
a lemon in the elm's sore clutch,
poor antiseptic for infection of its trunk
vectored by bark beetles
that bung it up with microfungi
until every single branch goes dutch.

The field boundary, once a well-laid hedge
that acted as rote syntax for the land,
now dies back more than a winter's worth,
blurting out indecipherable rules
in the interstices of sedge and sky —
without a soul to offer up, the tree can but
whisper to the mute, hermeneutic earth.

Film on the Skyline

The side-light is sepia
on February's ice, pyrite
for the film they're making
to fake time past —
rosy cheeks and screaming kids
in a city with roots and futures.

As if on a boom-arm, a full moon rises
criss-crossed by orange planes,
bubbles in a spirt-level
sizing up the tilting world
to balance a night not yet young
with late-life crises of the day.

The golden caryatids
of Saint Mary-by-the-Bourne
are bemused Oscars, posturing
as if they bear the clouds' grey freight.
Gormless in the face of the grating wind
they wait to be dedicated

not knowing what goes unfinished,
not watching the tea-time rushes heading west.
We want to believe the sunset is real
despite the loud hail on the east wind
directing us to frame the cold self-interest
of dreamers in a goldmine.

Echo Location

Tricking out the temerity to
talk back at the city's scheming hiss,
or its sister, teasing tinnitus,
I weaken at the first fussy trill
of a single spiralling ringtone –
never mind the gorging wheels screeching
or the screams of fleeing sneak-thieves or
the bankrupted neighbour's weasel words.

A nail in the floorboards called my name,
a shadow caught my biting eye, and
I sensed spirits in the corridor.
A curse of empty people peeping
into what's supposed to be a space all mine
but whose echoes now only locate
their own crowing biosonar souls —
and I'm the aural bailiff's repo.

Out on the streets, the yammering of
the jackhammer's incurious slog
courts the manners of wannabees, stuck
like itching dogs in their future's glitch.
And, at his pitch, the double-dealing
alley-Don's neon-lit, barefaced lie
mistakes you for a look-alike from
a rival gang in a bungled heist –

imprisons you in crack-fed furies,
where wimps in got-at juries fail you
and jail you, simply in your own self.
A penal-code poltergeist caught in
the striated headlights of sodden
roads, a mirage of a monstrance for
a mass of sound that won't abate, till
it's far too late to hear your way home.

Ancestry

Don't tell me any more to count
myself lucky for your pearls
of wisdom disappearing,
as they were shucked, into that limbo
I knew, where the bathwater you threw
away with the baby fed the stems
I plucked from the world — the work,
the company, the woman I loved
you said was a bimbo.

Don't fledge my days with hand-me-downs
now I can buy off-the-peg, nor try
to measure my success when you've half
a mind to disregard
it, like the tasks you said I'd left half-
done, when in fact I'd done them in half
the time — and still you tapped the table
with the fingers of your half-
remembered self.

Don't bother with your fingers,
the only counting being done now's
from staring at our genomes —
I'll get your number, then I'll get mine
and engineer a history
as cosy as you like. I'll spike
the veracity of inheritance,
each nuance you wanted to perceive
now merely a tick on a baby's face.

Don't number me amongst you.
Count the genes. Count them.
Are you man or worm?
Are you replicating as you squirm
or simply duplicating
the habits of your class?
Past masters out to grass
playing with daisies and passing the buck,
looking for luck in the chain.

The Petals in the Snow

As if velvet hurts, you said.
But there was more. More of what
you said would be nothing.
On frozen mornings velvet hurts.

Bits of the bloom you'd worn
in your hair last night lie on the violent
white, labelled for record, photographed
in situ, routinely taped-off from despair.

Velvet hurts, brutally removed
from inviolate flesh
dumped in a ditch to freeze.
Vile ice that knows, in spring,
violets will grow through
what you said would be nothing.

After the Wake

What rancour is it easy
to take away now she's been
taken, even as I take
to task her revisionists
for new-fangled yesterdays?

Into their planned tomorrows
I am called, as if a friend,
to come to family feasts
where flannel and camouflage
would try my patience to death,

even if my very death
hadn't really crossed their minds,
or a turning of the screw
not seemed right to let some blood —
spirit softened as a fruit.

Each lie is a lie enforced
by fancies at gatherings.
Lies of the powers that be
that have no power as soon
as their egos are defied

by kin who're as much in touch
as cowbells ringing across
a mountain cleft, or a bird
with a telemetric chin
carrying its hackers' weight.

Paradigm Shift

It's all come to nothing, this
world-in-the-palm-of-your-hands.
On a slatey Sunday morning,
when empty streets can't witness your distress,
the abandoned past comes gunning
with given-up ghosts, in the silent wake
of funny weather and silly money,
till the honey-trap collapses, witless.

The world is coming out of its ears.
A cracked bell butts in, its knucklehead chime
so way-off the hour that it's practically cast out.
Each cack toll is anarchy for day and night.
They mumble truths and lie together,
even as the sun's bones crumble.

Capo Palinuro
Named after the helmsman of Aeneas.
Location of sea-caves where divers drowned in 2012.

I kill the outboard motor
and idle into the Grotto of Blood,
legging red bacterial walls.
Gloss blueness in the backlit sea
brooks no hint of Saturday's gloom
when four lost souls churned up the murk.

Who profits from this wanton dive?
Palinurus, did you jump to be
the one life offered for the many?
When Somnus fooled you,
did you scoff, like these young men,
at the nous of other pilots?

Neptune took them, though no blog says so,
though papers don't record vile doom.
Don't grieve too much, you'll wake them.
You, Palinurus, placed too much
trust in the sky and the ocean's
Calm. You'll live naked and dead on
the sands of an unknown seashore.

I idle from the Grotto of Blood
legging the candlewax womb
past the scream of cliff-edge flora.
Primula, primula,
the outboard motor roars
into the azure

through sulphurous rock-thighs
delivering baby perfect, perfectly blue:
without the hue to live,
without the heart to die.
I know Aeneas, I heard you. I know
my body casts no shadow.
I'm born again into purgatory
with no-one to plead for the Sybil
to steer me from this cerulean dome,
no one to stop it bearing my name.

The Disposition of the Sun

How mulish we were
to fertilise the same thing
the same way
year after year,
never taking heed of whether
the light would last or die.

Vermin eat the gleanings
of a summer's seed
even as we murmur
about the many skills now lost,
crossing our fingers
for stalk and stem,
wishing for cultivars
from undiscovered gardens.
We ourselves breed only doubt,
robbed by the sun
in the light of day.

The moon's still drawing
moisture for what
struggles from the loam
but, in a bee-less season,
pollen from our meagre crop
blows away to blossom
in the less distressing light
of another land —
selecting out
new bloom or blight
from hybrids at the margins.

Live Streaming

Muffled mic. Unwilling lens.
Only fluid truths to tell.
Dregs of the deluge swill
beneath a hapless finch.
Other birds, once clever on the wing,
rest gingerly on severed
wire as sea conspires
again to lap the shore,
a shore dredged up by that waxing
range of obligate waves, shoaling.

Elephants return to ruin
that no one believed their sonar
foretold. From the ash of disbelief, false
gods rise for bereaved survivors toying
with telepathy and the hearsay
of good news as watertight as yesterday.

The wreck of the wave-train is waiting
to see who'll be brave in it,
who'll be the first to tell the world
that a ring of twisted stanchions
should be a henge for brand-new ancestors.
The dawn's last ditches feed
an acrid lake back to the sea
as I make out slow shapes in the coastal marsh:
no-one waves, they wander,
each group in another's undertow.

Straits of Messina

Agata stands, unadorned,
black to the ankles in a foaming lap,
foreshore-drunk. She peers
for traffic in the shipping lanes
revering him, not as her brave
protector, but as a nervous sailor
conscious of Odysseus' fear.

Prevailing winds are foreign.
All sailors speak in tongues.
Untranslating morning
has no word to borrow sail
and she must harbour her sorrow,
knowing that the freight
of absence also needs a hull.

The Cortex Coast

With this we wrestle:
  there is no skin of sky.
It has all become water

crushed by the pestle
  of the cliff, one lie
to the other in the mortar

of the grey-brimmed bay.
  We learn the differences
between white and black

in interchanging ways,
  each hemisphere influencing
dark contact

between carbon and the heart
  with contrast so blinding bright
it's melting the ice,

stripping the bark
  from a tree of life,
the stars from a deity's eyes.

The Medlar
After sonnet LXXIII

Count down my days and ravel the seasons
from burst of leaf to light, to dark, to dust,
as blossom's fire, lit beyond all reason,
tries to belie the temple-razers' lust.
Crepuscular on me, the hold of time
grows firmer with every setting sun,
wrapping tightly the fusc of night's design
on a world of sleep where the worldless come.
No. If you must look at me that way, see
orchards fruit anew from fertile ash,
jewels on every excarnated tree
where I once grew before life burned and slashed.
  You come for one last time, in frost, to blet
  the fruit that now gives up what none forgets.

The violet was flawed on the lawn

Elizabeth Bishop: 'A Cold Spring' from *North and South – A Cold Spring*

Still Frame

I see you as the moment freezes
looking in the mirror
staring at the far and near;

crying, trying hard to please,
but blinded by the manganese tears
of need and fear –

it cuts both ways, the unfaked face,
sight out of sight of camera shake.

So, I blink through the blistered lens,
framing only the hope that lies
beyond your eye's kaleidoscope;

winking away the mist for sense
in reflection that, with time, might
focus through the bogus mirrors and smoke.

Clytie
Bronze by GF Watts, V&A

Nine days on the lichen
pining for her loss
of Helios,
she metamorphosises,
twisted ever tighter
by the litmus
of her turnsole logic,
writhing
beyond art's torsion
as an unrequited gaze
suspends our disbelief
in her god of light.

Writing Down Passwords

I.
What of need
when I forget the letters
to tap on your breast,
the digits to slide on your thigh?

So what's what for a minute
isn't
and the threshold has a bell
not chiming with memory

just peeling in hope
that what does get remembered
is fast iron for a climber,
rope for a man deep down in a cave.

II.
Your secret is safe with me,
I can only whisper
with the breeze at a summer supper,
sated and grateful for company.

What I might divulge lies
somewhere between a spy's report
and the declension of a verb
given rote under torture,

a pledge of love now forfeit,
caught
in the crux of a black eye's blink
by a dreamer on the edge of bogland

who slayed a lord
that gods might praise his dream,
and might appease
the goddess of his master's worship.

In Exile

After all these years
we play meeting on a corner
we never ever knew,
pledging ourselves
to a game of seduction
that wants us to sashay
out onto a ledge
heady with hope.

Under the breath
you almost don't have,
you swear,
swear at being controlled
by the tryst
with this love grown large,
swear at being complicit
in the death of us,
swear about the doubters
for what they saw
as the meaning of our world.

They couldn't hear
the blessing in dissension,
they couldn't feel the weight
of that alpine mountain
beyond our bedroom window,
so heavy so light.
They couldn't hear your breath
as it redefined
the sense of weight,
so heavy so light
so heavy so light.

Above the Bay
Summer 1956

Far removed from the modern trap
Hughes's great bird fell in Benidorm
innocent of nesting —
or just cuckoo-like
with word-gestation for an ego
going for it, out of youth to manhood's quest
to better and not be bested,
up an' at 'em in the early works,
knowing how war could make and unmake men,
sensing mystery in the stillness of the raptor's eye
effortlessly: form as formerly dictated
now forgotten in the cadences
he knew the Movement wouldn't modulate.

Before satellites, *Puig Campana*:
he had to have stood on that ochre mountain
to be able to say he saw the bay
that way he did in Moonwalk,
not batting an eyelid
about leaving his bride
on a quay with fish, to her not terrible yet,
nets forever being repaired
in pinhole light through changing shade, awe
for the littoral still unashamed —
aiming his hawk at a shower of fame,
only to see the falcon falling, cadging no ride,
crash-landing in a craw of sea.

False Dawn

Anyway, you mean the opposite.
You mean things are different.
You mean we are and we aren't

meant never to be barking up wrong trees
stuck on the malarkey of genitives,
rendering out the peace from being,

soldering light onto blackness
too weakly to make the break of dark,
so morning is a prisoner of night

paroled and rearrested, fitted up.

I wanted to throw the heavens open
to sowers of seeds, to waxing moons and priests
but, for what the dawn and larks pretend,

I must hunt behind the scud of cloud
bending as a sunbeam to kiss your blood
through the prism of day's first weak delight.

Rail

Friesians in fog
piebalds in the plough,
embankment a couple of furrows
away from the dithering edge
of a world supposedly known.
And yet not known. The kale fields
are lost to cellophane scarecrows
on watch for petitioning souls
beneath the Fenland shroud.

Blackthorn's new white blossom
looks yellow against it,
over before pollination,
and then not even yellow
as the hedgerows are laid into grey.

In the blank frame of the window
half-blinded eyes sketch the chevron
lines of a pylon pulsing static
through the fret's hidden grid,
making me shy of the throb in my heart
making me hanker to be out of this void,
bidding me believe the byre in the field
can still offer shelter, with the rot
in its joists, and the moss on its planks.

Crux

In the dead of night,
a chill route back to you
lies barely perceptible
under the moon
in signposts of ice —
the trail was made
by feet in snow
and morning's warmth
will leave no path.

Divine Works
for Hildegard of Bingen

Heaven's mystery in plainchant,
or you, seated with slate and book,
given to your mandala of process in the cosmos,
its order in the swirl of winds.
Blessing earth with messages in Latin
from visions in your soul not seen with your eyes,
shedding your sadness as you lose
sight of yourself in the sight of god,
considering yourself as nothing
even as you're called upon to be more:
what membrane separates you from the light
whelming out of heaven with falling stars?
Plummeting angels hit the sea as blackness,
blind-spots from the phosphenes of your migraine.

Dawn in Accettura

Birds seethe
through the last
of last night's shadow,
through the hilltown's
eye-mask eyes,
into the soul
of the crown of the rock,
a Golgotha
waiting for the light dolled-off
behind the Mountain of the Cross.

Matins bells do not shed night
and mark no time.
In ragged competition
they don't arrest,
don't call the world to prayer
to pray for a world that shuns its calling —
the skull
awaits its flesh,
the birds their pick
and the hollows for their blood.

Here Was Castro
*Inscription erected by Pope Innocent X
after his forces had razed the town in 1649*

The rasp of automatic canons
agitates wolves descending with night
from Monte Amiata
to harry thin flocks
on the ignorant plain at Castro.

Castro. Castro, layered
on Rome and Etruria,
duchies, states and gypsyvilles.
Carthago of the Maremma
delenda est, delenda est
mending itself into green ravines
half-filled-in,
imploring still to know itself beyond
a papal curse, beyond lost
verses of Etruscan poets.

From the dusk of Dante's wood,
shrieks of murky birds hang
on the unsown terrain,
devil-may-care, resounding
from copse to cleft to unkind sky
warning that this place
of bullied bones and trove unlooted
interrogates itself each night, treasuring
its cold remains as gone
forever from the evil of life denied.

Open Season, Valdichiana

Birdbrained
in Cloudcuckooland's sun,
I curse a lack of Tuscan nous
as lead-shot burns the side of me
careening from an olive grove
to hunker by walls of broken querns.

No heave of life, just raptor-cry
and a hunter learning camouflage
anew, fledging invisible
out of the scrub, sack full of songbirds —
bread and butter for dignitaries and plebs
at small-town feasts where the women come
dressed to kill to ease the grind,
Venuses minus wreaths
catty for the hunters' bling.

Later on through the tick of night,
clean-cut figures sketch
themselves more vaguely, more prone
to the preening stretch, a little more oily,
hatching plots for new cocks-of-the-walk
if each was not himself a cuckoo's chick
who, in the thick of it, if it came to it,
couldn't say boo to a hoopoe.

But the hunter milled for his daily bread,
and, as if he'd given them hope,
as if his worth to them had risen,
the women come to feed him,

winnowing out what he doesn't need.
On the gunman's plate sit slender forms
plucked around the breast
still feathered where the limp necks dangle
at the edge, migrating to legend:
a shrill chorus begins to dawn.

The Moss House

I want to remember when
the green and yellow came fresh-cut
but the ancient turves have turned
again to worm and grass
putting me in my place
with the fallen beam of family
and the dregs of legend.
Doormat for Atlantic storms.

The soil on the promontory is salted
dead. Conniving angels pander
through lost window frames:
their eye on the berries
that grow by the sea;
their gaze on the farmers
so salt of the earth, whose fields
by default, are their cuckoo's nest.

Little of us remains material,
our pillars and tools were of wood
our clothes of beasts.
There's nothing but a keepsake carving
dropped at night inside walls now implied by
the edges of cracked floors beneath the sod.
Bulldozers tear omens
from hedgerows that no more enclose.

No revision of history here, no landlord's
mansion with a clatter of tiles.
Hard as the brain's excavation tries
roots entwine the door
to what transpired
and every insect takes down
a splinter preserved
picks out each last piece of home

from dissembling earth.
So you hurt no more
than you're already hurt,
and, weighed upon by prayers,
can no more remain
pretender to a mother church
than say farewell to settlements
where all are gone and none is known.

Sunday in the Bleached Piazza

Black against white light,
cathedral bells mimic transmitters
on the whitewashed rooftop
of a *Polizia* post next door.
Between the two, a skein of white bunting
bids us 'Welcome to the message of God'.

But whose communication counts?
Who turns the white lie into stone?
Will no-one intercede
on the side of the spied upon,
when one institution triangulates where you are
and the other one's Trinity wants you at Whitsun?

The Migrant
after Paradise XVII

Go from this hard place.
  Leave all you love most

and win over the margins
  where cardinal virtues

tell you you must toil.
  Climb another land's teasing

scree and master
  the disintegrating summit.

Live on what leaves a bitter
  taste until bitterness grows

sweet and there's comfort
  in the cold of the wild.

Go out of your mind.
  You are justified.

With no roof to hide
  you from the untied sky,

you are indivisible
  from light and air—

rise with a heave of the wind
  to believe again in your world,

whether its ice is ageing
  or whether its age is ice.

For all things change, making way for each other

Amphitryon in *Heracles* by Euripides

Acts of Love

Fingers. Questioning your belly.
Seeking facts in the very wile.

Finding an answer where none is.
At a loss to say how things lie.

Man and woman lie. Priest and nun
hoping for a god to nod to them, or to banish

their creed to a fickle coast. Tell me.
How I long for us to stay. Am I wrong?

But you saw the book by my bed
and a light from the boulevard caught

the look in your eye. On eggshells.
Imitating the need at your breast

with a petrified dream you couldn't wean to life.
Land child who must leave on the tide,

I dream of a duty that will call you back—
I know of the guilt that will keep you away.

Clouds at Snape

They are what they are till they aren't:
a castle, a hut, a thing with feathers
or a fact of life becoming a dream

careering on rocks after brief success;
eyes that peer at forbidden things
a stranger receiving a welcome home

a cringe in a hero, the butt of a joke
the pother of cumuli; coda, fugue
love's smithereens and flawless kisses

words for the wordless endlessly speaking
to the indigent iPhone down a ravine;
a light shaft sublime in Turner's book,

in Goya's hand, disasters of war;
belief in the grand and truth in the sick,
the brushstrokes' bend and swirl;

muscle on a girl or curls on a boy, the classy
and classless, till they are or they aren't
some craquelure in the self-same heavens.

At the Eye Hospital

When tears fall on dust,
dust is no more mundane —
what's not supposed to be beautiful
changes in refracting light.

Is this how I measure devotion?
Anything your tears touch
touches my soul, infecting me
synapse by synapse,
assuming control
of every brittle limbic fuse.

How do you demonstrate your love?
The chemistry of crying
is beyond experiment
and knows your every retort
will boil the mystery of fact
I lay before you.

When tears fall on dust,
notwithstanding the mist
they leave behind,
the eyes from which they fell
see far, grow visionary.

The Workers

He's been telling them till he's blue in the face
and still they make him jump through hoops,
reddening the arm of his grandad's coat
on a rusty edge of the wheel.

Dream of steel; dream of repair;
dream of a tailor in a naked land.

You can stall all you like, the boss was told
but what do you make of our warp and weft?
What's material beyond yourself
as you strike our feet while we stand our ground?

Jump to it, be still. Be here, be gone.
Do what you want but do my will.

We do as we must to survive, wary of trust
in liberal tongues. Snags have got to be grist to us—
we'll jump through those hoops till they are no more
and learn to sew up the threads of our rags.

The Secret of Evensong

What did I do to move you
to tears? Was it just my glance
that tied you to the prayer
I whispered as you panted
through the canticle?

What precious reputations
could get tarnished by the tryst?
You didn't hesitate to
say there'd be no harm in us
practising our faith,

and this song is my vicar
of desire for you, a trick
of role-play, of who believes.
You free my mind of duty,
teaching me of love –

or what I pretend lust is
in the unstormy calm of
the vestry's dusk, as the ring
of truth up in the belfry
overcomes our sighs.

Green Belt

I asked you on that day
when terror spiked, how

would you, because of the bomb,
because of the fire's bad air,

conduct their lightning
into your city's earth.

I asked you about life beyond
the pale and how we might

cross the freezing urban edges
where a map of plotted litter thins.

Wheezing knights patrol
these fringes, weighed down

by the chink of change, playing off
each other's stories of a war, dogged

by truth in their trade of secrets
for metal-bashing moneymen.

Warhorses, startle-eyed in the din
of their own alarms, snort toward

blind canyons, wise enough to carry
county to city till the city is earth again

and earth is all there ever is
in the city of your mind.

Writers in Marina Baixa

Roughshod sometimes
or persuaded,
the ridden rest on unprotected hills.
Not gilded by the setting sun
they weather away
restless for unrest again,
well-drilled in their belief
in dawn.

Scops owls suck their call
in the scrub clearing
of a tenancy
where the den of sky
can be built and struck
like a camp in an hour,
guards at the next stop overpowered
by the mendicants' right.

Wildcats and brooders,
whose ranges
don't respect this type of change,
give the sierra voice:
insistent gifts from feral fear,
until the night has no more will to speak
and only the restless
listen.

Nura

catchlights
of stars in your eyes
carry shadows
in their sparkle
appalling us
in our urge to think
that the precious baby
found wrapped in a shawl
is only a diamond
that comes with a curse

Heap Theory
re Sorites paradox

How time flies.
It seems like only this morning
they comforted me with
'You'll be fine in the home,
it's hardly as if you've lost your marbles.'
I know, I know. I'm using them now
on the theory of heaps:
one subsuming another
or assuming another's form,
the angle of every pinnacle
uncalculated and perfectly the same.
Don't get me started, but listen
you boys of the falsehood,
on what do you predicate
your judgement of age?

I keep saying I won't deny
there's a will to deny
I'm over the hill,
but this is for keeps:
I'll hold my head up on the crown
of the next heap's rise,
seeing whole worlds
from the hollow cell of my bed,
packing more into time
than lapses allow,
inventing more words for hill
than the Saxons had by the dozen.

By suppertime, I can't think back.
The once photographic is blank
and I settle by the gene-pool
in a trick of light.
Neither here nor gone,
there is no fact of the matter of what I am,

but there's a buzzard above,
so there is life down here:
ragwort, cornflowers, Doone Valley thyme;
fiddlehead fern and horseshoe vetch;
the gossamer wings of Adonis Blues
on candyfloss rhizomes at the wetland edge —
a sketch of beginnings and the menace of ends
vanishing by sunset as doves incant.

Chess Garden

In the over-wintered beds and paths,
devising a move toward spring,
topiary apes a gambit in calculating light.

Black, on the move in the parterre squares,
plays with silhouettes of blobs too madcap
to dress their robbed shapes with liveries of self.

And there, beyond the debris of the maze,
ripping weeds from a ha-ha, stooping workmen
become the manes of steeds for muddy knights —

such simple Sirs, conceding with reputations slurred,
hoist on bad petards under mossy castle walls
in the cause of the sundial bishop who demanded all.

White, the time-worn foe, fights evanescence.
With no line at all between haze and sky,
is history being revised by the pure and the bad?

Is that the innocent queen I see
on the fragmenting keep, not able to bring herself
to watch the fall of her rooks' bleak battlements?

Are those bound-up sticks young pawns
who took too big a risk? The drunken benches
on their ends the castled king they couldn't save?

Half-lost in this stalemate of form
pale buds hope to be promoted to flower,
but instead of the endgame they intended,

in the day's last hour, they meet sudden death
and thud to earth from a tree-surgeon's saw –
adjourning the season's compulsion to move .

Tea in Maine

for Marguerite Yourcenar...'nothing is slower
than the true birth of a man', Memoirs of Hadrian

Maybe it was reader's block,
but decades of praise for Hadrian's epistle
couldn't stop me feeling I had boxes to tick:
did he have any character at all;
was he the hero of his own life?
What of heroism for the author now
with Grace Frick dead, love and translation lost?
Quick in many tongues, the first woman
in the Academie francaise could be prickly
and, leaving Clifton Dock in midsummer fog,
I wondered how my questions might be greeted
at Petite Plaisance on South Shore Road,
the home of the lady I knew as Madame.

Maybe it was taking stock too favourably
but the more I itched to sound her out
the more closed the virtuoso became.
I knew that she knew that fiction communicates,
that time was her treasure and tea-time was time,
not time-out for tomfoolery with entente:
like the Memoirs, I was plotless, pricking balloons
till the Earl Grey stewed and the muffins were cold.

Maybe it was while I pretended to listen
to the next topic being fixed like a butterfly,
that I too felt brittle,
piqued with no mandate for rebuke.
Wriggling under her reputation's weight,

I took the used things to the kitchen and left
by the rear screen-door through a cloud of midges,
charcoal-black against white pyracantha
blossoming from half-inferior ovaries
to fruit red pomes in Fall.
Along Somes Sound, I grounded myself
on pink plutonic rocks, then skipped down to the sea
to try to wash away the sense of being belittled,
first as a human, and then, with a cold salt splash,
just as a male: beyond granite and semantics,
the roar of the Atlantic could not drown out
the rubric of an Emperor's lines.

To the Land of Punt
Elea (Velia) flourishing port
and home of the Eleatic school of philosophy

Each time I sail from Elea
Parmenides challenges me
to come to my senses, postulating
that merchants have no nose for truth.
But, true to myself, I get rich
on smell and taste, doing what I must
to bring the wild aromas home,
if home and love wait patient and safe
till I trade September for another spring.

Beyond blue river and red sea,
my caravan reaches Coptos
to tread as gingerly with strangers
as Egyptians had in the time of bronze.
Factors make short work of man's longing
for myriad riches: frankincense, gems, myrrh;
but mum's the word about the cinnamon's source
and even the pirates don't understand
they plunder the treasure of Taprobane.

'Come back again!' hangs daily on the wind,
while I burden my mules in Africa's Horn
but, knowing we might own what we didn't seek,
'Go home again!' is as often the rule.
Where you wait, Lucanians could conquer,
the crier in the square fall dumb:
in the absent musk of us, however hard,
stand firm on the crux of our unity -
tell Parmenides of riches that need no mule.

Conquest

Feathers fall from flight.
Bereft of dreams,
we're all still together.
No-one has left,

though the children
have seen stark hills
with boundaries lost
in the wilderness of tribes.

So what is the order
you insist you must impose
as some kind of basic right,
bordering on the fanatic?

It acts as a trap —
in the moment when you need to soar,
in the panic flap to get away,
feathers fall from flight.

A Spell For Green Corn

George Mackay Brown & Peter Maxwell Davies: Traditional

Verse for the Marshes

The wetlands of southern Iraq and their population
were systematically ruined in the late 20thC. Occupied
since Sumerian times, the ecosystem is now partially restored.

Is this the re-birth of my land
whose broken body bloats with salt
whose death-mask blisters in reeds of tinder
whose skeleton crumbles in the poisoned earth
of desiccated water-courses, once abundant
home held precious since Gilgamesh
regardless of custom, creed, tribe and cause?

What is my society's shrinking shape
hiding beside a Euphrates
hardly allowed to flow by dams upstream:
no groundwater in the ground, not enough
heart in the heartland of cities
to insist it matters that ways of life
should survive beyond a kingdom shattered?

No bedding for the buffalo, no pig
to hunt, no fish to spear, men of the marsh
abandon swamp for rectangular town,
but there's no Uruk there, no sane mother home.
What coracles now? What serpents?
How mythic these would-have-been-heroes
rootless beneath their deities' cosmos?

Saddam drained the spirit from an Eden,
yet in the geography, inundations murmur,
creatures come back from obscurity,
birdsong the litmus of their system's health.
From the chaos of Mesopotamian flames
scientists log taxonomies of every species
observed by well-remembered fishermen:

'Kaka-ki kaka-ki' the Basra warbler,
acrocephalus griseldis.
'Jee-ep jee-ep' the marbled teal,
marmaranetta angustirostis.
'Chiri-chik-chay' the Iraq babbler,
tirdoides altirostis.
The silence of the ibis, sacred *threskiornis*.

Sea of Jazz
The Waste Land was an 'agonised outcry of a sensitive romanticist drowning in a sea of Jazz' 1923 review.

Only the rag of sail works here
the chug of steam is out of coke

and brassy powerboats belittle,
kidding the ear to hear trombone —

but an alcove in the harbour bar
is a conch for music there to be found:

gangplanks, sailors, currents, fair wind,
high-hat trees on the shingle roof

rattle as the dots of a lazarus tune
jotted in the margins of a menu.

Solos blow in from the high sea's roar
through the scat of surf and feedback

of waves, signatures of time much further out
breaking the rhythms of the tide,

whose cool cats jive in a dinghy's wake
riffing on each atonal dive

returning through a vamp till cue
to rest on the dock's key octave —

flouting the sin in syncopation,
finishing at the sea-girls' perfect pitch.

The Place of Stones

from Aghaclogher, an Irish village name

The ether has emptied and seasons have gone, but winds
bless winds within themselves and stones are freed
with honing song. I am your ancestor, hewer of rocks,
these are my signals of home. I warm to the force
of this altered earth, how it prisms light from lough
and sky, configuring the land for indisciplined eyes.
This is the monument where memories reside, where,
to mark our worth, we barter with gods for excarnated
serf or corbelled king. It's where men cluster
from scattered farms, sharing their stories to the point
of trust. Pouring in from the cursus, their gatherings assert:
see us; know us; accept us. Exist and remember –
how beautiful we've learned how we came to be;
how beautiful the unknown, beyond the quag and scree.

Yawarra
Aboriginal track that leads from the beginning of time.

Tribesman,
you need to remind yourself why
you pissed in squatters' wells; why
you sometimes prised a slat from a selector's
roof to better let the winter in; why
you still have to suffer as a throwback
so they can bully their way
to a share of *terra nullius*,
disdaining your claims of invasion.

They roam gungho for land and water
with the blessing of Country and King,
just about able to remember Cook,
while you can dream back to the Pleistocene,
to the mythic dunes of Mungo Bay.
'Be father to your fortune' you mimic them
'but don't see the cuts on this son's face
as the scars of a lout: when the days are parched,
I'll find a spring in the desert's heart'.

Your kin become carrion just the same
through strychnine-laced flour
divvied out by under-handed bosses.
Piqued by loss of profit,
they thresh a failing crop
and cannot winnow what you yield
under the skin of broken lineage.
Ceremonies might end, memories die:
but myth is mountain; ritual is river;
faith is stencilled on the meeting-place stone.

Tribesman,
assert your origins.
The weapon of your ancestors is to warn
that what's taken by men with guns
cannot be possessed:
the seizure will come back to haunt them.
In your family's wake,
offer up the wings of birds;
breathe in circles at the ochred cave
with flowers in the rock — and stones
placed in rows beneath the gaze of a snake.

Butchery Lesson Before Easter

Last night, when owl-skirl
menaced the stick-edged copse
and sylph-mist kissed the lowlands;

last night, when bells fell
silent and man went home
to comfort or spleen;

last night, when skittish clouds
crazed across the moon's beam
to strobe my path through aniseed thorn;

last night, when I learned to split
the torso of the lamb
until the bones stood alone –

a spirit arose from innocent blood.

Behind a City Church

How to sponsor ideal things
when truth is as fickle as
weather, so quick to endorse
blind corners where tired men cheat:

scaffolding round the transept
moans in the mendicant storm;
tarpaulins billow up to
show the trash of self-abuse

glistening in spitting rain
under buttresses flying
off, as if undone by death,
to quit the unreal city.

So, undo yourself now too –
eros hides but is not lost
to town or moor. Go and feel
your way along secret walls

through all the stories of the
crowds. Shout out vibrant sequels
that speak of weeks of wonder
when evil doesn't flower.

Son Running

Asthma seems immaterial now
as I glimpse you on your morning run,
that well-worn kit quitting the carriage-
drive to sprint on slopes past the lake,

beginning to weave through trees as warp
and interlacing pathways as weft,
ready again to pick up the threads
of your life wherever new land looms.

You, the bobbin, rocking right and left
deft through every jammed adjustment,
making cloth of who knows how much worth.
You who are young enough to be owed,

who can shuttle poses without wrath,
who can fail and yet fall whole to earth —
stay bold in the face of lies and tricks
the fabric of your life enfolds you.

Puck Fair 1959

A wild goat is crowned and caged on a high platform.

Three squashed kids
in the back of an Austin
swamped by revellers ignoring the night,
pinned by feral eyes from the sky.
No vacancies.
Where on earth are we going to stay?
Dad inquires in Cahill's Bar,
but even he's too far from home
to meet the man he always meets in bars.

On MacGillycuddy's Reeks,
this king was already king, not a king-freak
with barely any ego left
to lord it over Killorglin's pagan chill.
Let's be still.
Perhaps there's a bed on his pedestal?

Lament from Euganean Hills

The waveless plain
  surrenders under cumulus
      sheeting down
          its leaden hail of warning:
don't
 mustn't
     shouldn't
        oughtn't
           can't.

Dark-skirted sign
  for me cadging rest, green actor
      alone on a muck-sweat bed
         anxious that dawn

won't be tragic, the thunder
 to thank for having no truck
     with the chorus of rain
        whose unison of fears I shun —
doubt
 hesitate
     suspect
       again and again
          never again.

       Is there a same mistake to be made?

And can I dream
  whatever I like in this
        deep wide sea of misery,
            the inaudible hymn

a paradise island,
  even you as an aqueduct
        for the torrent gathering
            to wash away defective verbs?

Tomorrow, in a new breath
        of life, I could propose
            we be conjoined —

but
  although
        unless
            as long as
                even if...

The Photos at Avebury

Me in the midnight-blue leather jacket
and the khaki Grace Kelly slacks,
you in the ritual behind your lens
for tomboy chic by a sarsen.

In between shots, you feather my skin
for its positive charge and I'm so in sync
that static's not static, just life let be
in the henge's pyschogeography.

Ancestors shield the existing hour
from threats of springtime Ridgeway rain
and we meander through stone avenues
circling each other, till our lust complains
beyond the honour of society's dues —
both of us electric, each new spark a flower.

Bats in Lucania

We bathed in the whole of the moon
and ran indoors to throw the shutters wide.
Warm enough to lie unclothed
I rested, certain of your silhouette
delicately folding us up into sleep.
A hand-wing in the *tenuta*'s beams,

we made safe our dark habitat
till that split second out of a dream
when your soprano screams rifled
the heart of our Basilicata night,
so sharp in panic at the pipistrelles
quivering above our limbs.

Moist again, you locked heels
on the master-bedroom's joist, spreading
your welcome in the moonbeam's fur,
the pitch of your call
commanding my mouth
until the mute fall of morning.

In The Morning...

we'll exit through a tongue of flame
licking at our histories
tempered by the violet fire
that shepherds our red dawn;

we'll exit through a tongue of flame
where a priest-moment burns,
shamanising
the fight to suspend our disbelief;

we'll exit through a tongue of flame
as new implements are tempered
for the chance of making up
what we never knew was meant;

we'll exit through a tongue of flame
bent as metal in our den of heat
each an anvil, each a smith
casting our innocence into the ash.

Juniper Dune

The high winds,
laden with sand and salt,
weld trees and bushes
into forms that mimic
the shape of the dune's
ever-altered state.

Capturing the sand,
each bush that comes
to grief develops
the dune's relief.
Every bleached branch
modelled in the winter sun

tumbles contorted
beneath the driven grains
that shift themselves
in time, to a standstill —
picturing land anew,
scumbling to be rock again.

Eve of Epiphany

Let out your breath,
it is done.

Climb the hill
to find there was no need,

other than greed,
to do a thing to prove your will.

Rather, as a bird
flung from the nest,

learn your skill by falling.
Hurl yourself from the crest

and take the wind
out of the world.

Acknowledgements

Thanks are due to the editors of the following publications where some of these poems have previously appeared: *Poetry Salzburg Review, Ink Sweat and Tears, Journal of Holistic Healthcare, Live Canon International Poetry Competition Anthology 2012 and 2018, Stone Anthology* (Wyvern Works 2012), *Hildegard: visions and inspiration* (edited by Gabriel Griffin for Wyvern Works 2014), *154 Poems in Response to Shakespeare's Sonnets* (Live Canon 2016) and the CD and permanent exhibition of the multi-media project *Rite of Cancer*. Other poems have been shortlisted or commended in the following competitions: *Live Canon International 2012 and 2018, Poetry on the Lake 2012 and 2015*. 'Sea of Jazz' won the *Wild Atlantic Words* competition in Co Cork, 2015.

THE HIGH WINDOW

The following collections are also available from our website, where further information will be found:
https://thehighwindowpress.com/the-press/

A Slow Blues, New and Selected Poems by David Cooke
Angles & Visions by Anthony Costello
The Emigrant's Farewell by James W. Wood
Four American Poets edited by Anthony Costello
Dust by Bethany W. Pope
From Inside by Anthony Howell
The Edge of Seeing by John Duffy
End Phrase by Mario Susko
Bloody, proud and murderous men, adulterers and enemies of God by Steve Ely
Bare Bones by Norton Hodges
Wounded Light by James Russell
Bone Antler Stone by Tim Miller
Wardrobe Blues for a Japanese Lady by Alan Price;
Trodden Before by Patricia McCarthy
Janky Tuk Tuks by Wendy Holborow
Cradle of Bones by Frances Sackett
Of Course, the Yellow Cab by Ken Champion
Forms of Exile: Selected Poems of Marina Tsvetaeva trans. by Belinda Cooke
West South North North South East by Daniel Bennett
Surfaces by Michael Lesher
Man Walking on Water with Tie Askew by Margaret Wilmott
Songs of Realisation by Anthony Howell
Building a Kingdom, New and Selected Poems 1989-2019 by James W. Wood
Out of the Blue, New and Selected Poems by Wendy Klein

Lightning Source UK Ltd.
Milton Keynes UK
UKHW022047181221
395882UK00009B/774